YOUR KNOWLEDGE HAS VALUE

- We will publish your bachelor's and master's thesis, essays and papers

- Your own eBook and book - sold worldwide in all relevant shops

- Earn money with each sale

Upload your text at www.GRIN.com and publish for free

Elisabeth Kuster

Twelve Angry Men (1957) by Sidney Lumet - an Analysis

GRIN Verlag

Bibliografische Information der Deutschen Nationalbibliothek:

Die Deutsche Bibliothek verzeichnet diese Publikation in der Deutschen National-
bibliografie; detaillierte bibliografische Daten sind im Internet über http://dnb.d-
nb.de/ abrufbar.

Imprint:

Copyright © 2007 GRIN Verlag GmbH
Druck und Bindung: Books on Demand GmbH, Norderstedt Germany
ISBN: 978-3-656-62628-2

This book at GRIN:

http://www.grin.com/en/e-book/182968/twelve-angry-men-1957-by-sidney-lumet-
an-analysis

GRIN - Your knowledge has value

Der GRIN Verlag publiziert seit 1998 wissenschaftliche Arbeiten von Studenten, Hochschullehrern und anderen Akademikern als eBook und gedrucktes Buch. Die Verlagswebsite www.grin.com ist die ideale Plattform zur Veröffentlichung von Hausarbeiten, Abschlussarbeiten, wissenschaftlichen Aufsätzen, Dissertationen und Fachbüchern.

Visit us on the internet:

http://www.grin.com/

http://www.facebook.com/grincom

http://www.twitter.com/grin_com

SE Ethical Issues in American Medical and Legal Narratives

Twelve Angry Men
(Sidney Lumet)

Stundent: Elisabeth Kuster

Handed in: 10th June 2008, SS 08

Contents:

1) Introduction

In this paper I will look at the film *Twelve Angry Men* (1957) by Sidney Lumet. In short the

film is about a criminal case in America in which a young Hispanic boy is accused of killing

his father and the twelve members of the jury have to decide on his verdict. In this case

"guilty" means death. After talking about the film in more detail I will also look at the jury

system in America and discuss some of its most important aspects, e.g. jury selection,

possible verdicts or the principle "Burden of Proof". In doing so, I will raise questions on how

fair the jury system really is and what its weaknesses or points of criticism might be. I will

then also discuss the various roles and duties of jurors and I will include ethical problems they

might be confronted with in their deliberations. Furthermore, the question if a jury is capable

of reaching a fair and legally correct verdict will be discussed and being looked at from

different perspectives. To conclude this paper I will show why the jury system, despite its

controversial position, is still used and probably will never be abolished.

2) The Film – Twelve Angry Men

2.1. Plot

Twelve Angry Men was released in 1957 and it was directed by Sidney Lumet. He was born in

1924 in Philadelphia, Pennsylvania, USA and until today has made more than 40 films. Many

of these deal with socio-political topics – so does *Twelve Angry Men*. This film was a huge

success and thus also nominated for various film awards including the Oscar and the BAFTA

film award. In the online film database IMDb.com it is ranked 12th on the list of the 250 Top

Movies. This implies that the more the 50 years old film is still popular nowadays.

(IMDb.com)

As briefly mentioned in the introduction the film deals with the deliberations of a jury in a

capital murder case. The person accused is a young Hispanic boy who is being charged with the murder of his father. After the oral pleadings of the lawyers the jury is asked to retreat and decide the verdict. The twelve jurors have to agree on the verdict unanimously which means they all have to vote for either "guilty" or "not guilty". At first the case seems to be open-and-shut: the defence cannot provide a strong alibi and there are various witnesses who claim to have heard screams, seen the boy running away and even seen him stabbing his father. Also the knife which the boy claims to have lost is found near the murder scene. From this short court room scene the film switches to the jury room where the rest of the film is set. After some unimportant small talk and a refreshment break the jurors (only men) gather around the table and take a preliminary vote – eleven "guilty", one "not guilty". Juror 8 (we are never given the names of the jurors) played by Henry Fonda says he cannot vote for guilty because he has reasonable doubt. At first all other jurors do not understand juror 8 and want to force him to change his opinion. But by presenting his reasons of doubt juror 8 manages to convince one after the other that sentencing this young man to death by the electric chair is not the right decision. He questions the evidences and alludes to the jurors' prejudices and weaknesses in order to point out that "it is possible" that he is "not guilty". After spending the afternoon in this rather small and gloomy room the jurors finally unanimously decide on the verdict "not guilty". They jury goes back into the courtroom and clears the accused of all charges. In the final scene we see the jurors leave the court building, only two of them exchange their surnames and then also part to go back to their lives (IMDb.com, *Twelve Angry Men*).

2.2 Characters

Just like a real (American) jury the film also consists of twelve major characters: juror 1 – 12. Each of them will now be described and interpreted. In the film there are no names given, the jurors are only identified according to their seating order.

Juror 1: He is the jury foremen who is responsible for the organisation of the decision-making process and also takes the votes. He appears to be a rather simple man and he seems not to be aware of the full complexity of his task but he is trying hard to hide this fact from the other jurors. The only thing we find out about his personal life is that he is a football coach and we only see him to be calm when he talks about football.

Juror 2: He is a small and quiet man. He thinks of himself that his opinion is not of much importance. This attitude may be due to his job – he is an accountant.

Juror 3: He probably is –besides juror 8- the most important and developed character in the film. Starting off by presenting him as a successful self-made businessman he analyses the case by looking at the mere facts. He is confident that convicting the accused is the one and only right decision. But after some time he seems to become more passionate and somehow also personally involved in the case. At the end of the film we find out that he has a son that he hasn't seen in two years. Looking at a picture of him and his son, he finally –as the last juror- changes his vote to "not guilty".

Juror 4: He is a slightly arrogant broker. He considers himself to be more intelligent than anyone else in the room and has a rather cool approach to the case. He sees the case as some logical science and ignores people's feelings and passions. It is very striking about him that despite the hot day he never takes off his jacket and does not even sweat – this can be compared to his attitude towards the case.

Juror 5: He always seems to be under emotional stress. He is the only one among the jurors who it not Caucasian – he is Hispanic just like the accused boy. Even though it might be unwillingly he identifies most with the boy. Strangely enough this is the main reason why he

votes guilty in the first place because he does not want sympathy to influence his decision.

But in a way it still does, just in a reverse way.

Juror 6: He regards himself as a simple man and implies that everyone in the room might be

better qualified to make difficult decisions than him. He is worried to make the wrong

decision, especially when it is a matter of life and death, but actually he wants to see justice

done.

Juror 7: He is the only juror who has absolutely no opinion on the case. Throughout the film

his thoughts are everywhere else but on the case, he talks about baseball, about the hot

weather and other things that are of no importance to the case. His only interest is to speed

this debate up and leave as soon as possible. That is why he just assents to the vote of the

majority, he does not bother whether the boy is cleared of all charges or convicted.

Juror 8: He is the main character in the film. He is the one who has reasonable doubt on the

accused boy's guilt and therefore puts more effort and thought into the case than anyone else.

By picking out key points in the case, like the knife or the statements of the witnesses, and

thinking them through again he raises doubt in everybody else and after some time manages

to convince all other jurors that it is possible that the boy is not guilty and that this reasonable

doubt is enough to not convict him. In a way he is the one who saved the boys life.

Juror 9: He is by far the oldest jury member. Because of his age he has the most experience he

has a very unique way of looking that the case. He is also willing to discuss the case again

instead of leaving instantly.

Juror 10: He is the racist character in the film. He votes for guilty only because of the boy's social background and worst thing about him is that he does not even want to hide his racist attitude.

Juror 11: He is an immigrant watchmaker and as his watches he is very methodical. He is also very polite and shows good manners by respecting the different opinions of people. He is also willing to look at both sides of the coin. The only person he can not deal with is juror 7 because of his indifferent behaviour.

Juror 12: He is a young business man and appears to have his own opinion on the case but is careful to hide it. He considers it to be more intelligent to just agree with what the majority think.

From this short characterisation of every juror in the film it can be seen how difficult it is to make a decision when so many different people with different attitudes and different opinions come together. In real life this problem is the same. Later in this paper, I will discuss some issues of the jury system, the duties of jurors and the responsibility they have to carry especially also regarding the tagline of the film – "Life is in their hands, death is on their minds" (IMdb.com).

3) The Jury System in the USA

In America about a quarter of a million people are called for jury service each year. Jury duty therefore is something that can happen to anybody, even to you. But it should still be kept in mind that jury trials, despite that seemingly large number of jurors, are exceptional events in the American legal system. They represent only 1 per cent of cases in State courts and 2 per cent in Federal courts (Parker). But once trial by jury has been decided the jurors' task is to

find a verdict for accused persons and so decide on their freedom or livelihood. The question

that might sound quite intimidating to everyone is how they find you and why they chose you

to condemn someone to death when there are so many other people. But once you have been

selected as juror it is your utmost duty to try your best to do justice (Lehman). It is significant

that a criminal crime jury exemplifies the constitutional principle that nobody should be

imprisoned or suffer a penalty for a crime unless they have been found guilty of committing

this crime by their peers. The jury decides its verdict only on the facts of the case and

therefore they can decide hard cases without making bad law. The jury system also requires

members of the public to gain an insight into the administration of justice and into

understanding the legal and human rights. As Thomas Jefferson, 3rd president of the United

States, already put it the jury system is "the anchor which holds a government to its

constitution" (Hostettler, 9).

The jury system also is a highly controversial matter, as it can have strong supporters on the

one hand but on the other hand also some strong opponents. According to Hostettler, a jury

system like that provokes passionate comments. They say,

> Twelve individuals are chosen at random, often with no prior contact with the courts,
> to listen to evidence (sometimes of a highly technical nature) and to decide upon
> matters affecting the reputation and liberty of those charged with criminal offences.
> They are given no training for this task, they deliberate in secret, they return a verdict
> without giving reasons, and they are responsible to their own conscience but to no
> one else. After the trial they melt away into the community from which they are
> drawn.

The problem that arises is the discussion on how democratic or anti-democratic the jury

system nowadays is. There is a friction between doing justice based on common sense, legal nihilism and innate feelings of what is right or wrong and doing justice based on the concept

of justice represented by the state and the law (Hostettler). This friction further leads to an

ideological and ethical conflict, which will be discussed in more detail in the following

chapters.

3.1. Selection of Jury

The Sixth Amendment of the United States Constitution provides that all accused have the

right to a speedy and public trial by an impartial jury in criminal cases. The Seventh

Amendment guarantees the right of a trial by jury in civil cases when the value of controversy

exceeds twenty dollars. It is interesting however that the main body of the Constitution as

passed did not mention a general right to trial by jury (Abadinski).

Traditionally a jury consist of twelve persons. Reasons for the number are unknown, it is

speculated that it is based on the Biblical twelve prophets and twelve apostles. The recent

trend in the United States also permits juries with less than twelve members. As of 1976

twenty-six states allowed this establishment (Brody).

Jurors are selected randomly from a fair cross-section of the society. The first step is to draw a

panel of possible jurors. This is called venire or juror pool. This panel is usually chosen from

the voter's registration list or from other sources like driving licence holders or tax rolls,

depending whether it is a federal or state court. The second step is to narrow the numbers of

people in the venire in order to select the twelve jurors for the case. This process is called

"voir dire". Its purpose is to find an unbiased and representative jury. In this stage, the panel

is being asked questions in order to find out who is biased, related to the case or prejudiced. If

any of these reasons apply, jurors can be excluded from the service "for cause" (ucsd). Each

side can also exclude a certain number of jurors (two to six) from the panel without naming any reasons. The Fourteenth Amendment states jurors are not allowed to be challenged or excluded because of their race or gender (Clack).

The question now to be asked is if this is a fair system to select a group of people who are then summoned to decide the fate of an accused person. Of course, an argument for it is that there is the "voir dire" process to exclude some people, but on the other hand it is not guarantee that the final twelve persons are capable of fulfilling this rather difficult task. From my point of view this has many reasons.

First of all the jurors are all laypersons. They are not used to court proceedings and supposedly not very familiar with the law in general. In my opinion they are not able to see how valid a certain piece of evidence is or how important a witness is. Therefore they can only judge from their feeling what is right or wrong. So the question here is whether a group of people with no expertise in legal actions are the right ones to be responsible to make decisions that could change or sometimes even end a life.

The second problem I see lies within the "voir dire" process. The jurors are being interrogated by the lawyers of each side and of course each side wants to win the trial and the first step to do so is to find a jury that is in favour of them. So already the selection of jurors is biased as lawyers could try to indoctrinate the jury to cultivate friendly relationships with individual jurors (Abadinsky). Therefore the "voir dire" does not guarantee that the accused receives a fair trial with an impartial jury. This issue of and impartial jury is also mentioned in the film *Twelve Angry Men* when Henry Fonda, juror 8 says:

> It's very hard to keep personal prejudice out of a thing like this. And no matter where you run into it, prejudice obscures the truth. Well, I don't think any real damage has been done here. Because I don't really know what the truth is. No one ever will, I suppose. Nine of us now seem to feel that the defendant is innocent, but we're just gambling on probabilities. We may be wrong (Medill).

And also by looking at the various characters in the film it can be seen that a jury probably is far from being impartial or unbiased and often they are not aware of their responsibility in the case. For example, there is juror 10 who is a racist and there is juror 7 who does not care at all if justice is done, he just wants to get out of the court building. And I think this was not a cinematic idea to choose jurors like that, I think it is very likely that the film reflects reality. Even after the "voir dire" process you can never be sure that the best people for this task have been chosen.

The third and last point I want to mention is the issue of racial inequality in juries. As mentioned before jurors are drawn out of a pool made up by the voter's registration list. In 1999 Home Office research showed that about 24% of black people, 15% of Indian origin and 24% of ethnic minorities were not registered on the electoral roll and therefore are not eligible for jury duty (Hostettler). It is also rather shocking that until 1966 in many states were not allowed to be jurors even though they were registered on the electoral roll. Black people are also only allowed to be jurors since the 1965 Civil Rights Act (Medill). I think especially in cases where ethnicity, religion and gender play an important role there should also be jurors of the same group. The aim of the jury selection is to find a jury of peers and not fiends. By achieving that the chance that the verdict is decided on prejudices should be lowered.

To sum it up I would like to mention that in my point of view the jury system is a good and fair way to find a verdict. At least twelve people have to agree on the verdict and it is not just decided by the judge himself. But on the other hand it should also be considered if the so called "jury of peers" really is that its name implies.

3.2. Role of the Jury During the Trial

During the trial the jury only has a passive role. They have to listen to the case and the

evidence provided by the opposing attorneys. Their final decision should then only be based

on the facts presented. The jury is not allowed to ask questions either to the witnesses or the

judge and they are not supposed to take notes during the trial. This practice has no

constitutional reasons but is merely the tradition of American courts. However, in recent years

judges tend to accept questions from the jurors in order to involve them in the judicial

proceedings. But jurors are not allowed to just pose the question in the middle of the trial

because the attorneys should be given a chance to object to some questions before the witness

is asked. Further, some judges also allow them to take notes during the trial (Hostettler).

Another important part is the instructing of the jury. Normally, this is the job of the judge. He

has to explain the meaning of law and how the law is applied. In order to avoid an appeal

jurors take great care that the wording is technically and legally correct. These instructions

have to contain some basic elements. The jurors have to be informed about the crime with

which the accused is being charged and also have to be given a range of possible verdicts. The

judge also has to remind the jury that the accused is presumed innocent and that the burden of

proof (see next chapter) is on the state. This means that if after hearing all evidence there is

still some reasonable doubt left, the verdict has to be not guilty. This is exactly the case in the

film "Twelve Angry Men". It is again Henry Fonda, juror 8 who puts it into words:

> We may be trying to return a guilty man to the community. No one can really know.
> But we have a reasonable doubt, and this is a safeguard which has enormous value to
> our system. No jury can declare a man guilty unless it's sure. We nine can't understand
> how you three are still so sure. Maybe you can tell us (Medill).

Finally, it also is the judge's duty to inform the jurors about procedural matters. That includes how to contact the judge if they have questions, the order in which they must consider the charges and who has to sign the official documents that express the verdict of the jury (Hostettler).

Concerning the role of the jury during the trial I have to pick up an argument again that I have already mentioned before. In the previous chapter I was talking about the jurors as only being laymen in legal actions. They have to be instructed and informed by the judge about all legal actions and procedures during the trial in order to follow the case. The question I ask myself is how someone who is obviously over challenged with the juridical system is entitled to decide a verdict. And then after this probably information overload during the many hours of a trial without having the possibility to ask questions or take notes, the jurors have to decide whether someone is guilty or not guilty.

3.3. Burden of Proof

It is always the plaintiff's or state's duty to prove that the accused is guilty of his or her charges. It is always the suing party who has to present all evidence to substantiate all allegations. This duty is called the "Burden of Proof". Therefore the plaintiff or state have to be the first ones to present the evidence and establish the facts. It is up to them to convince the judge or jury of the truth of their claims and thus of the guilt of the accused person (Brody). If they fail to do so the accused person is not guilty. This is what happens in the film. In the film's case the jury finally decides that there still is reasonable doubt left and therefore they clear the boy of his murder charge. However, the term reasonable doubt is not defined. Reasonable doubt defies quantification, but infers a degree of certainty that is conclusive and complete. It is however, less then certainty since that would be an impossible thing to ask of a

human tribunal (Abadinsky).

The duty Burden of Proof seems to be a very fair concept to me. It is also similar to the Latin

maxim "in dubio pro reo" which means "benefit of doubt". Those two rules convey that an

accused has to be acquitted if there is doubt left. The only problem is that you need a judge or

jury who question and take a closer look at what seem to be facts. In the film all evidence

presented in the case seems to be clear-cut. And if it was not for juror 8 nobody would have

questioned that. But as doubt is raised more and more aspects come up that prove that not

every piece of evidence is as important or clear as it may seem on first sight.

It think for a jury it is very crucial to decide what piece of evidence is determining. Of course,

with new technologies which are available nowadays many things can be proven scientifically

through e.g. DNA analysis. Such pieces of evidence can then be taken as watertight. But in

many cases such evidence is not available. This is where the jury's job gets more difficult. In

many cases witness statements are considered to be important. How can someone tell that a

witness is more honest and reliable then the accused person? A witness could also have

reasons for not telling the truth and just because they are sworn in and instructed to tell the

truth it is no real proof that this is what they really do. So I am not sure if a witness statement

is enough to fulfil the duty "Burden of Proof".

3.4. The Verdict

After both sides have presented the case and all evidence the jury has to retire to the seclusion

of the jury room to deliberate the verdict without outside contact. The verdict has to be

reached unanimously. Sometimes this decision making process takes a couple of hours and

the jurors have to be provided with food and sleeping accommodations until they finally come

to an agreement. Even though the jury has to deliberate in privacy they may request a clarification of legal questions from the judge and they are allowed to look at items of

evidence and even at parts of the case transcript. However, they are not allowed to look at

anything else, for example law dictionaries. It is also not possible to get the opinion of an

expert on the discussed matter. It can also still happen that the jury deliberates in all good

faith for many hours but they are still not able to agree on a verdict. In such a situation the

judge can declare a mistrial. This means that a new trial may have to be conducted (Clack).

Research studies show that most juries come to an agreement fairly quickly. It is common

practise to take a first vote after retiring to the jury room in order to see how the opinions are

divided or united. In 30% of all cases it only needs this first vote to reach the unanimous

decision. In 90% of the remainder, the majority of the first vote wins. Hung juries – those

with no verdict, occur only rarely (Clack).

If the jury agrees on a verdict, they are conducted back into open court where the jury delivers

their verdict to the judge. Also the opposing parties are informed of the verdict. Usually the

members of the jury are then asked individually if they agree with the verdict. This is done to

find out if each juror really agrees on the verdict or if he or she just followed the verdict

because of group pressure. If it is revealed during this polling that the jury is not of one mind,

it is sent back to the jury room to continue deliberations (Clack).

Actually I find it rather outstanding that most juries come to a verdict that quickly. Of course

this could either mean that the trial was well presented and that no procedural errors were

made or it could also mean that the jury does not look close enough at the case. They just

decide on what on the surface seems to be certain without thinking about it a second time.

This might again be due to the fact that most jury members are not familiar with the law and

therefore do not even know how to question a certain piece of evidence. I think they probably

need another impartial "supervisor" that always presents them with both sides of the coin. I

am also not sure if it is justifiable to not allow legal dictionaries or more material where the

jurors could get background information on the legal procedures. In my point of view one should make sure that jurors despite the fact that they are laymen in deliberating a criminal case should at least be given the chance to decide the verdict to their best knowledge and belief.

3.4.1. Jury Nullification

To highlight the difficulty of finding a verdict and the options jurors have I chose to explain the jury nullification in more detail. The jury nullification is also a verdict that causes controversial opinions. "Jury nullification occurs when a jury returns a verdict of "Not Guilty" despite its belief that the defendant is guilty of the violation charged. The jury in effect nullifies a law that it believes is either immoral or wrongly applied to the defendant [...]". By nullifying the jury also ignores the judge's instructions on the case (Linder). I will now look at arguments for support of the jury nullification and at argument for opposition to this very special verdict.

People in favour of nullification claim that it protects an accused from the government. They say that sometimes even evidence and guilt is not enough to justify a sentence. In their eyes it is a benefit of the system that brings law and community closer and also adds a new dimension to the concept of democratic self-rule in the jury experience (Hostettler). I think especially the second argument is important. The jury system was invented to avoid a verdict decided by one single person and so make the trial in general more democratic. By giving jurors also the possibility to decide against the judge's gives the system an even more democratic character.

Those against nullification mostly claim that it is illogical, unlawful and untidy. Many people even believe that such a verdict is only reached when the jury feels intimidated by the accused. In their eyes it is "folklore" (Hostettler, 147) that liberty until the present day depends upon a jury. By saying this they actually are not only against nullification but they are criticising the jury as an institution. Further, they believe that jurors will always be on the side of civil liberty and only an academic lawyer can decide on the right verdict (Hostettler). Of course there is also truth in their arguments, but sometimes judging by law leads to a morally wrong sentence. So what is still in the dark for me is if it is right to reach a verdict on the basis of the correct legal procedure or can that be ignored when a deep moral conflict with the accused and his or her sentence occurs. I think it can.

4) Conclusion

After presenting some central key points of the jury system in the USA and after raising "reasonable doubt" on how effective and fair the system really is I would like to explain why the system has persisted for so long and why it is a valuable cornerstone in American legal system until today.

Despite the fact that the jury system has often been criticised throughout history it has always stood firm against being eliminated. They system got strong through tradition and it withstands all doubts because it is the only area where the people can interfere with the administration of law and because it is a tool to mitigate legal doctrines that are otherwise implemented by a judge alone. It is a "government of, by and for the people" (Lehman, 339). All that enables the society to stay in a much closer contact to the law as would otherwise be possible. On the other hand, there is still the question whether a judge is not at least equally or even more capable of evaluating evidence. Juries are inconsistent in applying and understanding legal principles and therefore trials by jury are cumbersome, time-consuming and expensive (Brody).

The most probable reason why a jury is still an intact institution is that it diminishes corruption and it preserves the purity of both, the jury and the court (Brody).

To sum it up, after considering all facts of the jury system and bearing in mind its controversies I believe that it is an institution that should persist. It makes the court and legal principles and procedures more democratic than if it was "ruled" by only one person, namely the judge. This however means that for every trial it does not only require a jury that is aware of their duty and is willing to do justice but it also needs a judge that is skilful and impartial. Only if these two work together on the best possible basis for a fair trial can be guaranteed.

Bibliography

Abadinsky, Howard. Law and Justice. An Introduction to the American Legal System. Saddle

    River, New Jersey: Pearson Education Inc., 2003.

Brody, David E. The American Legal System. Lexington, Mass.: Heath, 1978.

Clack, George. Outline of the U.S. Legal System. Washington DC: Bureau of International

    Information Programs, United States Department of States, 2004.

Hostettler, John. The Criminal Jury Old and New. Winchester: Waterside P, 2004.

"Jury Selection." University of California, San Diego. 31 May 2008

    <http://psy.ucsd.edu/~hflowe/jursci.htm>.

"In Search of a Fairer Jury Selection Process." Medill Journalism. 31 Aug. 2004.

    Northwestern University. 30 May 2008

    <http://docket.medill.northwestern.edu/archives/001433.php>.

Lehman, D. Godfrey. We the Jury…The Impact of Jurors on Our Basic Freedoms. New York:

    Prometheus Books, 1997.

Linder, Dough. "Jury Nullification." 2001. University of Missouri-Kansas. 31 May 2008

    <http://www.law.umkc.edu/faculty/projects/ftrials/zenger/nullification.html>.

Parker, Stephen. Legal Ethics and Legal Practice. Oxford: Clarendon Press, 2003.

"Twelve Angry Men." Internet Movie Database. 30 May 2008 <www.imdb.com>.

Filmography

Twelve Angry Men. Sidney Lumet. Orion-Nova Productions.1957.